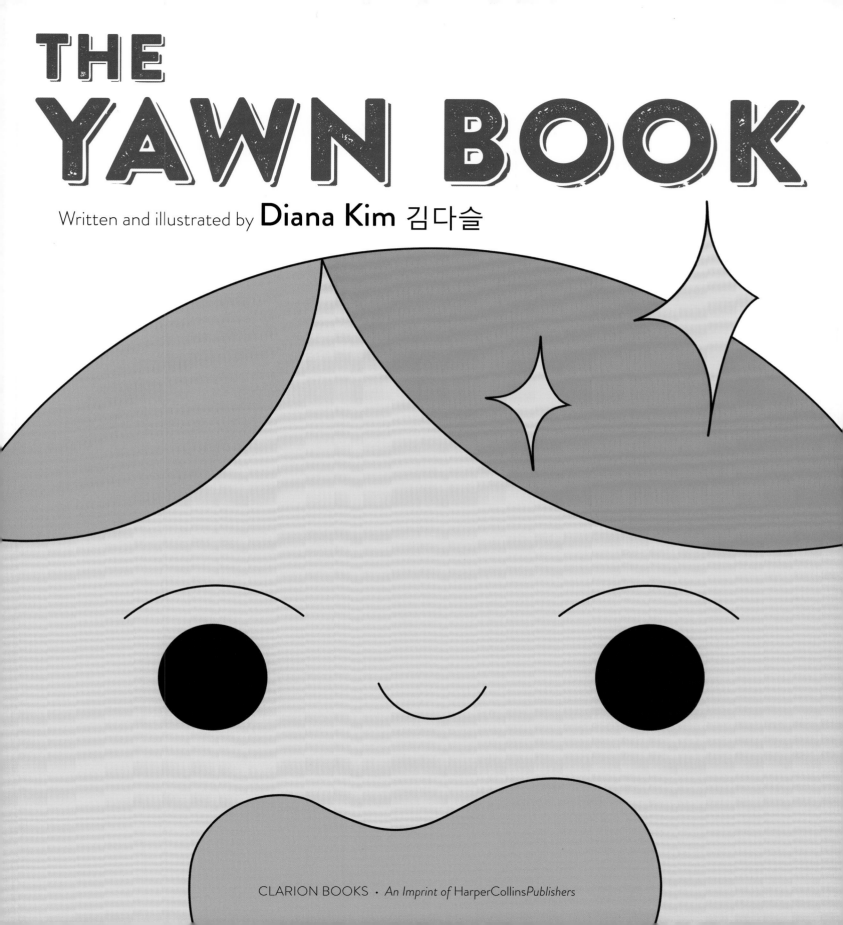

THE YAWN BOOK

Written and illustrated by **Diana Kim** 김다슬

CLARION BOOKS · *An Imprint of HarperCollinsPublishers*

It all starts when we are young and small.

A human baby growing in the womb begins yawning at 12–14 weeks. Yawns can be seen on an ultrasound, which produces images of the baby moving.

Yawning is something we do all our lives,

Babies yawn an average of 30 to 50 times a day.

The amount that **children** yawn increases as they learn how to read and write. Elementary school–age kids yawn five times more than kindergarten-age kids.

but the amount we yawn may change as we grow.

Adults yawn an average of 20 times a day.

Older people tend to yawn less than younger people.

How often we yawn doesn't only change with age. It also varies throughout the day and night.

We yawn most during the hour before bed . . .

. . . and the hour after we wake up.

Otherwise, we often yawn when we are bored, tired, or hungry. But not always.

You may feel like yawning when you are trying to focus or have a job to do. For example, musicians may yawn before an important performance.

Scientists have studied when we yawn
and how much we yawn . . .

. . . but they still aren't sure WHY we yawn.

Some people believe yawning helps us move from one state of mind to another. That would explain why we do it when we're waking up or calming down!
?
?

There are many different ideas about why we yawn.

Perhaps yawning cools the brain by bringing cold air into our bodies?

What we know for sure is that yawning is contagious! People can "catch" a yawn just by hearing someone else do it. Or even by reading about it!

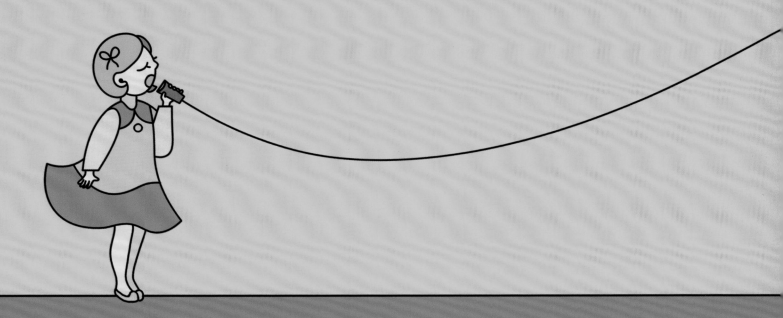

Some theorists believe that contagious yawning is a form of communication. They think we yawn to show empathy toward others—to show we understand and share their feelings.

Are you yawning now?

We are more likely to yawn when someone
we feel close to is yawning.

Someone in our family. Someone we love.

Even your dog!

Yes, animals yawn too. At least, those with backbones do—mammals, reptiles, amphibians, birds, and fish.

A single **lion** yawning can make the rest of the pride, or family, yawn too.

Some **penguin** species, including the Adélie and emperor, yawn as part of their mating rituals.

Some **snakes** yawn to realign their jaws after a meal.

Guinea pigs may yawn as a sign of aggression.

Fish may yawn to take in more water to get more oxygen and keep their gills clean.

No, bugs don't yawn.

Even with all these theories and observations, what exactly makes us yawn continues to be a mystery.

Could you be the person who solves the mystery?
It all starts with one question . . .

Why did you yawn while reading this book?

Sources Cited

Aguirre, Claudia. "Why Is Yawning Contagious?" YouTube video, uploaded by TED-Ed, November 7, 2013. www.youtube.com/watch?v=4NpG4F9yq00.

Allen, Keiron. "Are Mammals the Only Animals That Yawn?" *BBC Science Focus.* www.sciencefocus.com/nature/are-mammals-the-only-animals-that-yawn.

Barton, Adriana. "Fetal Yawning: Cute, But What Does It Mean?" *Globe and Mail,* November 21, 2012. www.theglobeandmail.com/life/health-and-fitness/health/fetal-yawning-cute-but-what-does-it-mean/article5535237.

Breus, Michael. "The Surprising Details Behind Yawning." *Sleep Doctor,* August 17, 2017. thesleepdoctor.com/2017/08/17/yawning.

Bryner, Jeanna. "Yawns More Contagious Among Friends." Live Science, December 7, 2011. www.livescience.com/17365-yawns-contagious-friends.html.

C, Tian. "Excessive Yawning in Babies—Is It a Concern?" FirstCry Parenting, September 26, 2018. parenting.firstcry.com/articles/excessive-yawning-in-babies-is-it-a-concern.

Carey, Teresa. "Why Are Yawns Contagious? We Asked a Scientist." PBS News Hour, July 17, 2018. www.pbs.org/newshour/science/why-are-yawns-contagious-we-asked-a-scientist.

Davis, Emily. "Why Do Guinea Pigs Yawn?" Clever Pet Owners, November 12, 2020. cleverpetowners.com/why-do-guinea-pigs-yawn.

Dell'amore, Christine. "'Contagious' Yawning Occurs More Among Loved Ones." *National Geographic,* December 5, 2011. www.nationalgeographic.com/science/article/111213-contagious-yawning-health-science-empathy-evolution.

DeNoon, Daniel J. "Why We Yawn." WebMD, September 23, 2011. www.webmd.com/brain/news/20110923/why-we-yawn#1.

Fuller, Mark. "Capturing Fish Yawns." Dive Photo Guide, January 17, 2013. www.divephotoguide.com/underwater-photography-special-features/article/photographing-fish-yawns.

Giganti, F., and P. Salzarulo. "Yawning Throughout Life." *The Mystery of Yawning in Physiology and Disease,* edited by O. Walusinski. Karger, 2010. www.karger.com/Article/Pdf/307072#:~:text=Intheelderlythefrequency,themorningandmidafternoon.text=Thetimecourseofyawningdiffers,functionofage%5B5%5D.

Hadley, Debbie. "How Do Insects Breathe?" ThoughtCo, July 12, 2019. www.thoughtco.com/how-do-insects-breathe-1968478.

Johnson, Jon. "Why We Yawn and What It Means." Medical News Today, July 15, 2017. www.medicalnewstoday.com/articles/318414.

Koerber, Brian. "The Science Behind Yawning Will Exhaust You." *Mashable,* March 13, 2014. mashable.com/archive/yawning.

Konnikova, Maria. "The Surprising Science of Yawning." *The New Yorker,* April 14, 2014. www.newyorker.com/science/maria-konnikova/the-surprising-science-of-yawning.

Rhodes, Tim. "What Does It Mean If My Guinea Pig Is Yawning? (Tired & Sick?)" My Pet Guinea Pig, January 3, 2022. mypetguineapig.com/guinea-pig-yawning.

Sample, Ian. "Yawning in Womb Could Be Used as Baby Health Indicator." *Guardian,* November 21, 2012. www.theguardian.com/lifeandstyle/2012/nov/21/yawning-in-womb-healthy-babies-2.

Samuelson, Kate. "Why Is Yawning Contagious?" *Time,* June 8, 2017. time.com/4801522/is-yawning-contagious.

San Diego Zoo Wildlife Alliance, "Lion: *Panthera leo.*" animals.sandiegozoo.org/animals/lion.

Schier, Mark, and Yossi Rathner. "Why Do We Yawn and Why Is It Contagious?" Medical Xpress, May 21, 2018. medicalxpress.com/news/2018-05-contagious.html.

Singer, Oliver C. et al. "Yawning in Acute Anterior Circulation Stroke." Abstract. *Journal of Neurology, Neurosurgery & Psychiatry* 78, no. 11 (November 2007). www.ncbi.nlm.nih.gov/pmc/articles/PMC2117604/#:~:text=Healthyindividualsyawnabout20,0%E2%80%9328perday.

SnakeTracks. "Do Snakes Yawn?" March 25, 2020. www.snaketracks.com/do-snakes-yawn.

Valdesolo, Piercarlo. "What a Yawn Says about Your Relationship." *Scientific American,* January 31, 2012. www.scientificamerican.com/article/what-yawn-says-about-relationship.

Wildlife Informer. "Why Do Snakes Yawn? (The 4 Main Reasons)." wildlifeinformer.com/why-do-snakes-yawn.